TOULOUSE-LAUTREC

MOULIN ROUGE

PETITE ENCYCLOPÉDIE
DE L'ART

© FERNAND HAZAN, PARIS 1958
DROITS DE REPRODUCTION RÉSERVÉS MUSÉE D'ALBI
PRINTED IN FRANCE

TOULOUSE-LAUTREC

MOULIN ROUGE

BY

ÉDOUARD JULIEN

TUDOR PUBLISHING CO.

NEW YORK

Once released from the discipline of the studios of Bonnat and Cormon, Lautrec set off joyously to find new and really living subjects in the Moulin Rouge and the cabarets of Montmartre.

It was in the heart of that turbulent and never-ending spectacle that the artist was to find the atmosphere and the subjects most suited to his genius; it was there that he was able to develop to the full the gift for the portrayal of character and movement already evident in his earlier drawings. He set to work with a will: "In the cabarets and balls of Montmartre," Joyat tells us, "always seated in the same place, so as to command the same angle of vision, he became a legendary figure."

Though the glittering world of festivity and entertainment which he portrays was a source of inspiration to many other painters in the great days of the Butte, none of them was ever able to re-create it with the verve and realism of Lautrec, a born portrait-painter, who allowed none of its essential elements to escape his pitiless pencil, and with a few rapid strokes achieved an irresistible and definitive synthesis.

Plate 1: MOULIN ROUGE. POSTER. 1891.

As Cheret's poster of 1889 was now out of print, Zidler, the founder and manager of the Moulin Rouge, had the happy idea of asking Toulouse-Lautrec, a regular customer whose talent he appreciated, to design a new one. He had reason to congratulate himself on this decision. The poster, in which La Goulue and Valentin-le-Désossé are shown in action, appeared all over Paris with sensational effect, and Toulouse-Lautrec's name became a household word. Thus his triumphant career as a lithographic artist opened with a remarkable sucess. From the very beginning Lautrec showed a complete mastery of this form of art—a form which he was destined to rescue from the mediocrity which threatened to engulf it. The thirty-one works which bear his signature deal with a variety of subjects, but are all alike in the exceptional power of the drawing and painting.

Plate 2: LA GOULUE AND VALENTIN-LE-DÉSOSSÉ LITHOGRAPH. 1887.

This famous dancing team made its début at the Moulin de la Galette. It was Valentin who "discovered" his future partner. His own career had begun at the Bal Mabille in 1866, where he danced for his own amusement. When his wine-business in the neighbourhood of the Halle au Blé was expropriated, he became a clerk in the office of his brother, a solicitor. He always wore the same shiny, dented top-hat, drain-pipe trousers, and frock-coat, while the ungainly movements of his inordinately long arms and legs earned him his sobriquet, "the Boneless" (le Désossé). His picturesque, legendary figure could not long escape the pencil of a Toulouse-Lautrec.

Plate 3: LA GOULUE AND HER SISTER. COLOURED LITHOGRAPH. 1892.
This is the first of Lautrec's coloured prints.

Louise Weber, a washerwoman from Alsace, began her career as a dancer at the Moulin de la Galette, and later became the principal star of the Moulin Rouge, under the name of "The Glutton" (La Goulue). Later, when she was too old to dance, she appeared as an animal-tamer in her own fair-ground circus at the Foire du Trône. Lautrec decorated the canvas walls of her booth with dancing scenes.

Plate 4 to 6: YVETTE GUILBERT.
—Painting on cardboard. *Pushkin Museum of Decorative Arts, Moscow.*
—Charcoal drawing touched up with colour. *Albi Museum.*
—Lithograph.
Lautrec attacks the famous popular singer relentlessly, portraying her character with a lack of indulgence not far removed from caricature. He has shown her every attitude, her every fleeting expression on every stage on which she appeared. With her thin hands and arms hidden by long black gloves, she had sung at the Jardin de Paris, the Moulin Rouge, and the Divan Japonais, and had made an enormously

successful tour of America. The songs which
made her famous were composed by Maurice
Donnay.

Though she had deigned to approve the
portraits of her painted by Frappa, Bach
Blanche, and Bellery-Desfontaines (all well-
known artists of the time), she had never liked
any of the numerous drawings of Lautrec, who
had met her in 1891; she said they were "hor-
rible" and called their creator "a little monster".
As a result, he usually refused to show them to
her. Yvette would not allow Lautrec to print
the poster he had submitted for her approval,
doubtless influenced by her adviser, Jean Lorrain,
who claimed that it was a "hideous distortion."

LA BUVEUSE - WOMAN DRINKING. DRAWING. 1889.

The lithograph showing Yvette Guilbert in "The Bird-Lime" ("La Glu", Pl. 6) is the second plate in an album, *Yvette Guilbert,* with a text by Gustave Geffroy, illustrated by Toulouse-Lautrec, and published by André Marty in 1894 in an edition of a hundred numbered copies, signed by Yvette Guilbert, and containing sixteen plates. It was sold at the time at fifty francs a copy. A second album containing eight lithograph portraits of Yvette Guilbert, with a text by Arthur Byl, was published in 1898 by Bliss and Sands in London. It was only after long hesitation that Yvette Guilbert could bring herself to sign Lautrec's lithographs which satisfield neither her nor her family and friends; they, indeed, advised her to sue the artist. But if her name is still remembered, it is mostly in connexion with him.

Plate 7: ARISTIDE BRUANT AT THE MIRLITON. POSTER. 1894.
Aristide Bruant had been a great friend of Lautrec since 1888, and exercised a considerable influence on him until 1892. A former official of the Chemins de fer de la Compagnie du Nord, he had begun writing songs while still at school. After singing at the Ambassadeurs and the concerts of "l'Époque", he opened a cabaret, *Le Mirliton,* in the Boulevard Rochechouart in 1895, where he welcomed his guests with chaff and mockery. The cabaret of this "Homer of the faubourgs", as Léo Claretie called him, who expressed so well "the pathos of the dregs of the people" (Anatole France); when he sang popular,

sentimental, slangy songs in his "arrogant and brutal voice" (Jules Lemaître), was patronised by a distinguished clientèle of writers, painters, and actors: François Coppée, Lucien Guitry, the future Edward VII, several Grand Dukes . . . The works of his friends adorned the walls, Lautrec's occupying an honourable place; and. the artist also contributed drawings to the newspaper *Le Mirliton,* which was sold at ten centimes a copy during the show. Lautrec has recorded the unforgettable figure of his friend in his 1892 posters for the Ambassadeurs and the Eldorado; and in the plan, now on view in the Albi Museum, of a large and impressive, but unfortunately never executed work. Bruant also appears in a number of other drawings and paintings.

Plate 8: THE ENGLISHMAN OF THE MOULIN-ROUGE. COLOURED LITHOGRAPH. 1892.
This is the second coloured print engraved by Lautrec in 1892.

Mr. Warrener was a regular customer of the Moulin Rouge on his frequent visits to Paris, and it was there that Lautrec made is acquaintance. The artist, who spoke English and was attracted by Warrener's obviously English features and carriage, found him an interesting companion.

The painting in the Albi Museum, *Portrait of Mr. Warrener,* is a study for this print, and shows how much careful preparation preceded the final version of Lautrec's lithographs.

LE CHANSONNIER - THE SINGER ARISTIDE BRUANT.

Plate 9: JANE AVRIL LEAVING THE MOULIN ROUGE. OIL ON CARDBOARD. 1892. *Wadsworth Atheneum, Hartford, U.S.A.*

Plate 10: JANE AVRIL FROM THE BACK. OIL ON CARDBOARD. *Albi Museum.*

Plate 11: JANE AVRIL DANCING. 1892. *Louvre Museum, Paris.*

In the first of these plates, Jane Avril is shown leaving the Moulin Rouge, where she has just been dancing. Near her can be seen the English painter Charles Condor, an habitué of the music-hall, and friend of Lautrec. Although she looked like a "mournful rat", Jane Avril had inherited from her father, an Italian nobleman who had fallen in love with a Parisian demimondaine, an undeniable distinction and aloofness of manner, so that "in the street, she might have been taken for a school-teacher." She had had a difficult childhood, which had permanently affected her health; in her slender build, and her delicate nature, as well as in her education, she formed a complete contrast to La Goulue. Before becoming a dancer, which had been her ambition since childhood, she had been obliged to accept a post as cashier in a shop in the Rue du Caire, and later worked for a short time as a circus rider at the Hippodrome. In 1890, she at last made her début at the Moulin Rouge where she danced with La Goulue in the famous naturalist quadrille, but soon left to appear as a solo artiste at the Jardin de Paris, the Décadents, and the Divan Japonais.

About 1900, she came to London, before setting off on triumphant tours in the French provinces and America. She then returned for a while to the Moulin Rouge, and was also to be seen among the beautiful skaters at the Palais de Glace. She married the illustrator Maurice Biais.

Plate 12: THE FEMALE CLOWN. PAINTING. 1895. *Louvre Museum, Paris.*

This painting, bought for 5,000 francs by the famous collector Isaac de Camondo, forms part of the valuable collection which he bequeathed to the Louvre. The dancer Cha-U-Kao, here shown dressed as a clown, is the subject of several paintings and drawings by Lautrec. One such portrait is in the Oskar Reinhart collection at Winterthur, and another, a very fine one, in that of Mr. and Mrs William Powell, at Gate Mills, Ohio, U.S.A.

Plate 13: MAY BELFORT ON THE STAGE. LITHO-GRAPH. 1895.

May Belfort, an Irish singer, had made her début in London, before coming to Paris, where Lautrec noticed her. She appeared at the Eden Concert, the Jardin de Paris, the Alhambra, the Parisiana, the Décadents, and the Petit Casino. She would come on dressed in a short frock of only one colour, affecting to look and act like a baby girl. Carrying a cat in her arms, she would sing, phlegmatically, with only a few restrained gestures, and in English, her hit song,

"I've a little cat". Her health was delicate, and she had to retire from the stage when she was still young. Lautrec devoted many drawings, lithographs, and paintings to her, and she is the subject of a famous poster, which she had commissioned for her performances at the Petit Casino.

Plate 14: THE CHAP BOOK. POSTER. 1896.
This poster, designed to advertise the American magazine of the same name is also known as *A Scene in the Irish and American Bar*. This bar, which the painter knew well, had been founded by an Englishman, Reynolds, at no. 35, rue Royale, next to the famous Weber. The bar-man, Ralph, who can be seen on the left of the picture, was held in high esteem by the customers, who included English jockeys, coachmen to distinguished families, writers, and a few café-concert artistes, among them May Milton and May Belfort, who sometimes had supper there. The latter appears in Lautrec's litho-graph: Miss May Belfort at the Irish and American Bar.

Plate 15: "CHOCOLATE" DANCING. GOUACHE. *Albi Museum.*
"Chocolat, c'est moâ!" It was with this catch-phrase that the placid negro who partnered the famous clown Footitt drew a laugh from the spectators at the Nouveau Cirque as soon as he entered the ring. He quickly attracted the attention of Lautrec, who used to meet him in

YVETTE GUILBERT BOWING TO HER PUBLIC.
c. 1894. *Museum of Art, Providence, U.S.A.*

the Irish and American Bar, to which the clown repaired as soon as his act in the circus was over. There "Chocolate" would dance, and sing a popular song of the time, "Sois bonne, ô ma chère inconnue" for the amusement of the customers. He appears in Lautrec's series, "At the Circus", where he is shown sitting balanced on the back of a chair playing the banjo.

4

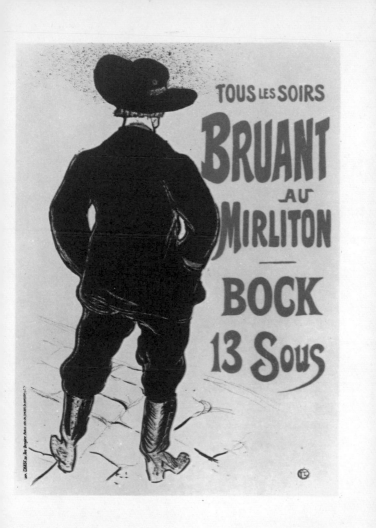

TOUS LES SOIRS

BRUANT
AU
MIRLITON
—
BOCK
13 SOUS

7

8

9

13

ACHEVÉ D'IMPRIMER
EN FÉVRIER 1958 PAR J.-M. MONNIER
CLICHÉS PERROT ET GRISET

DEMCO